# The Happiness Book For Kids

## A Kid's Guide To Happiness!
## Volume I

Mike Duffy

Copyright © 2014 Happiness Publishing

All images courtesy

of 123RF.com

All rights reserved.

ISBN-13:978-0692315408

# DEDICATION

I dedicate this book to my incredible family including my beautiful wife Shannon, my gorgeous daughter, Kendall and my wonderful son, Michael.

Feeling happy is fantastic! In this book you will learn the secrets to happiness. Try one every day. These secrets will give you a lifetime of joy and happiness!

## Choose To Be Happy

Happiness is a choice. Throughout each day, you can choose to be happy or you can be choose to be sad or angry. Choose happiness each time!

## Be Positive

Try to always think of good thoughts. Have a "Can do" attitude. Imagine yourself being able to do anything and everything you want to do. People love positive people!

# Make A Game Out Of It!

Make a game out of boring things like chores. See how fast you can do them and try to do them faster tomorrow. Have a chore contest with a brother or sister.

## Be Grateful

Always say, "Thank You!" Treasure the small things, like a breakfast made by someone you love or a hot shower.

# Enjoy Being You

There is only one of you in the whole wide world! You are a precious and special person. Don't try to copy everyone else. Be the best you can be!

# Be Kind

Help a friend tie their shoes. Hold the door open for your teacher. We are all God's children. Be kind and you will always be welcomed wherever you go.

# Forgive

Life is too short to hold grudges. Give people a second chance. You will never be perfect. That's okay! Forgive others and yourself.

## See The Silver Lining

When you are going through a tough time, it is hard to be excited about what good could come out of it. There is always something to learn from every experience, good and bad. Try to see the good.

# Take Care Of Your Body

You must love yourself and your body. Overeating, drinking sugary drinks, and not getting enough sleep are bad for your body. Eat healthy foods. Your body will be happy you did!

## Set The Right Goals

Noble goals, like serving and helping others, will lead to happiness. Change the world one person at a time. Be a force for good!

# Be Content

Having more stuff will not make you happy. Are you bored with toys that you had wanted so badly before you got them? Make your own toys and games. The rules are up to you! Being content is a big secret to happiness.

# Read

What do you like to do? There are books and websites written about your favorite things. Read about your interests. Reading makes your brain happy!

# Try New Things

Try new foods. Try new games. Try new silly dances. You'll never know if you like something until you try it. There is a whole new wonderful world waiting for you to try!

## Be A Good Kid

Good kids get rewarded! Bad kids get punished. Time-out stinks! So be a good kid and you'll be happier.

# Exercise

Exercise boosts energy, improves mood, controls weight, makes you healthier, and helps you sleep. Play games that make you run and jump.

## Be Confident

You are an incredible creation! Believe that you can do it. You will have more fun and have less fear, if you are confident.

# Laugh More

Don't take everything so seriously. Laughter makes you happy! A good belly laugh makes you feel so good. A case of the giggles is just what the doctor ordered.

## Smile

Smiling is contagious. Turn that frown upside down and everyone will follow you. Smiling gives you a happiness boost!

## Say, "I Love You"

Parents, grandparents, brothers and sisters need to hear you tell them that you love them. Tell them why you love them, too! Let them know how much they make you happy.

# Give

It doesn't matter if you don't have any money. You can give someone a hug that is crying. Give a nice compliment to someone. Tell a parent that they look great today!

# Let It Go!

Don't let disappointment ruin your day. When something bad happens, move on and do the best you can going forward. Understand that setbacks happen to everyone.

# Develop Talents

We were all given special gifts. It's up to you to find out what you are good at. Start with things that you enjoy, like playing sports, making music, drawing or dancing. Try to get better everyday at the things you like. Before you know it, you'll be great!

# Acknowledgements

I would like to thank all of the people that have shared their wisdom with me including: Dr. Fred Luskin, Dr. Laura Delizonna, Deepak Chopra, Tal Ben-Shahar, Shawn Achor, Dan Gilbert, and Zelig Pliskin.

Mike Duffy is the founder of Happiness Publishing, LLC. He has been researching happiness for over 29 years. He is the author of *The Happiness Book For Kids: A Kid's Guide To Happiness! Volume I & II* and *The Happiness Book For Little Christians: A Biblical Guide To Happiness!* and *The Happiness Book For Men: A man's Guide To Happiness*. He loves to speak about how you can gain greater happiness and joy in your wonderful and precious life. His audiences include corporations, universities and organizations. Mike is the founder of The Happiness Hall Of Fame. The Happiness Hall of Fame recognizes, encourages and celebrates people that through their talent, hard work and sacrifice make other people happy. www.happinesshalloffame.com

# Credits

All of the wonderful photos are from 123 RF.com. A great thank you to the following artists:

John McAllister© *123RF.com*

Liliya Kulianionak© *123RF.com*

Anthony Totah© *123RF.com*

Tatiana Katsia© *123RF.com*

Daniela Jakob© *123RF.com*

Stephen Bures© *123RF.com*

lightwise© *123RF.com*

Susan Richey-Schmitz© *123RF.com*

Judith Dzierzawa© *123RF.com*

iofoto© *123RF.com*

www.ingramcontent.com/pod-product-compliance
Lightning Source LLC
Chambersburg PA
CBHW041753040426
42446CB00001B/20